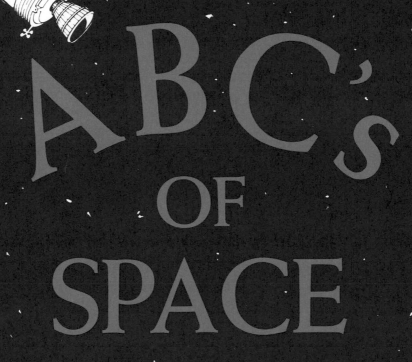

ABC's
OF
SPACE

ISAAC ASIMOV

WALKER AND COMPANY

New York

First published in the United States of America in 1969 by Walker and Company, a
division of the Walker Publishing Company, Inc.

Published simultaneously in Canada by The Ryerson Press, Toronto.

Library of Congress Catalog Card Number: 73-86406.

Printed in the United States of America.

Book designed by Lena Fong Lueg.

ACKNOWLEDGMENTS

The publisher is grateful for permission to use the following photographs and illustrations

The American Museum of Natural History
Pages 27, 32

Avco Missiles, Space and Electronics Group
Page 19

California Institute of Technology and Carnegie Institution of Washington
Pages 21, 40-41

Mrs. R. H. Goddard
Page 45 (right)

Erwin T. Handel, Crescent Art Service
Pages 31, 47

Lee Kleinberg
Page 13

Mount Wilson and Palomar Observatories
Pages 22 (left), 30, 34

National Aeronautics and Space Administration
Pages 4, 5, 6, 7, 8, 9, 10, 11, 12, 14, 15,
16, 17, 18, 20, 22 (right), 23, 24, 25, 26,
28, 29, 33, 35, 37, 38, 39, 41, 42, 43, 44,
45 (left), 46, 48 (left)

Wide World Photos
Pages 36, 48 (right)

Photo Research: Eleanor B. Feltser

To the memory of Willy Ley,

astronaut of the mind

To commemorate the successful landing

of the first men on the Moon,

Command Pilot Neil Armstrong and Edwin Aldrin, Jr.,

July 20, 1969,

with their companion in Apollo 11, Michael Collins.

A is for Apollo

a huge American spaceship that took three men near the Moon. It carried a smaller ship, the Lunar Module, in which two men landed on the Moon.

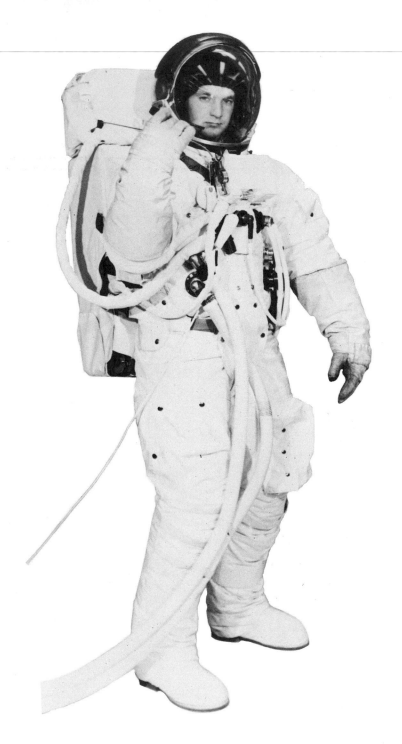

a is for astronaut

_____

_____

_____

a man in a spaceship that goes far out from the Earth.
He can walk in space. He can go to other worlds, explore
them, and come back. Americans and Russians are both
sending men into space.

B is for Biosatellite

a man-made satellite that carries plants and animals into space. One kind is called an "Astrobug," and sometimes it is nicknamed "Noah's Ark." By studying how the plants and animals get along, we learn how to make it safe for men on flights into space.

b is for blockhouse

a small, strong building near where the spaceship starts
to move upward. The people inside the blockhouse make
sure everything is going well. Thick walls protect them
from being hit in case of an accident to the spaceship.

C is for Command Module

the separate little room in which astronauts live while in space. It is at the top of the Apollo spaceship. From there the men control the rocket engines and all the other equipment. There they also make tests to learn about space and about the Moon. At last it brings them back to Earth.

C is for countdown

getting ready to send the ship into space. First the hours are counted, then minutes, then seconds: 10, 9, 8, 7, 6, 5, 4, 3, 2, 1, **fire**. If something seems to be going wrong, the countdown stops until everything is working right again. Then it is: "All systems go to lift-off!"

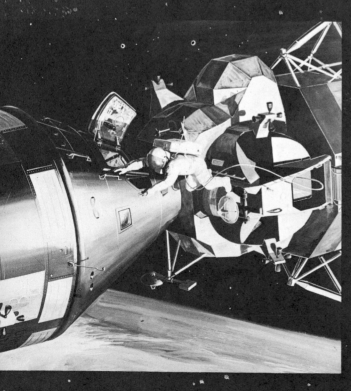

D is for Docking

two spaceships joining. When two ships
are near together in space, one can use
short rocket blasts to come even closer.
Finally, the two spaceships hook together.
They have docked. Then the astronauts
can climb from one ship to the other.

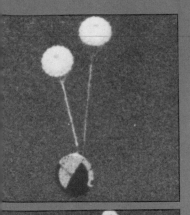

d is for drogue parachutes

_____

_____

_____

the first two parachutes that are put out, high in the sky, to keep a spaceship steady on its return to the Earth. Then three small white pilot parachutes are opened to slow it more. And finally three ringsail parachutes bring it in for a landing at sea.

E is for Earth

the large and beautiful world we live on. Astronauts
move so far away from the Earth that they can see the
whole side that faces them. It looks like a big round ball
in the sky, covered with clouds. Part of it is in shadow.

e is for exobiology

the study of life on other worlds. We do not know what this life is like—or even if there is any. But if there is, it will probably be nothing like Earth life. People have imagined many different ways it may look.

F is for F-I engine

the most powerful United States rocket engine using liquid fuel. Five of them are fired together to launch Apollo, or start it into space. The F-I engine is used to help get men to the Moon.

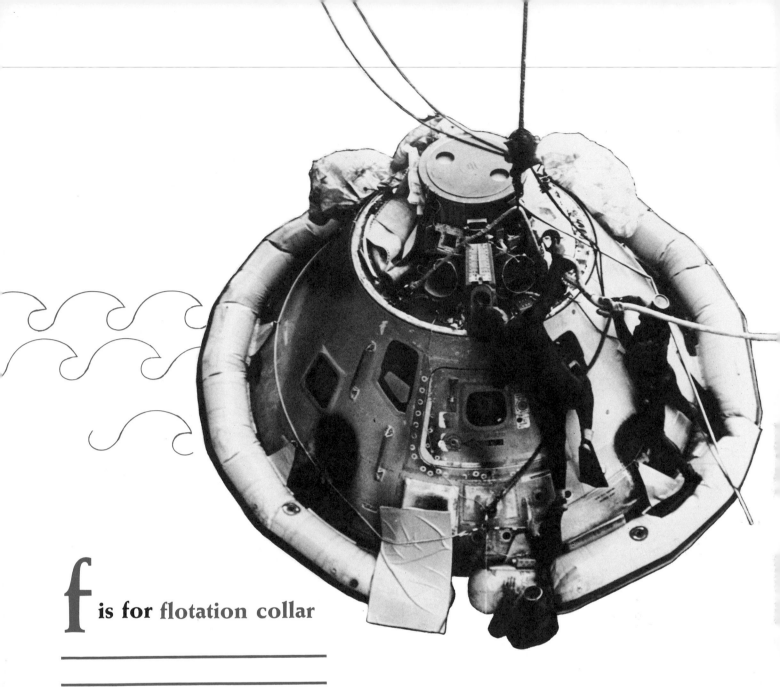

f is for flotation collar

_____

_____

_____

a large tube that frogmen place around a

spaceship after splashdown. It is full of

air, like an automobile tire. This keeps the

spaceship from sinking so that the

astronauts can climb out and be picked up

by helicopter. The spaceship can then

float until it is taken to land to be studied.

G is for Goldstone "210"

the biggest and most sensitive antenna to
receive radio signals from space. It is as
tall as a twenty-one-story building. It can
follow spaceships as far as they go, even
16 to Pluto, the most distant planet.

g is for gantry

a tower next to the rocket. It is a tall, movable building with elevators and instruments. Men use it to reach all parts of the spaceship. Astronauts go up in it to reach their places in the ship before it is launched.

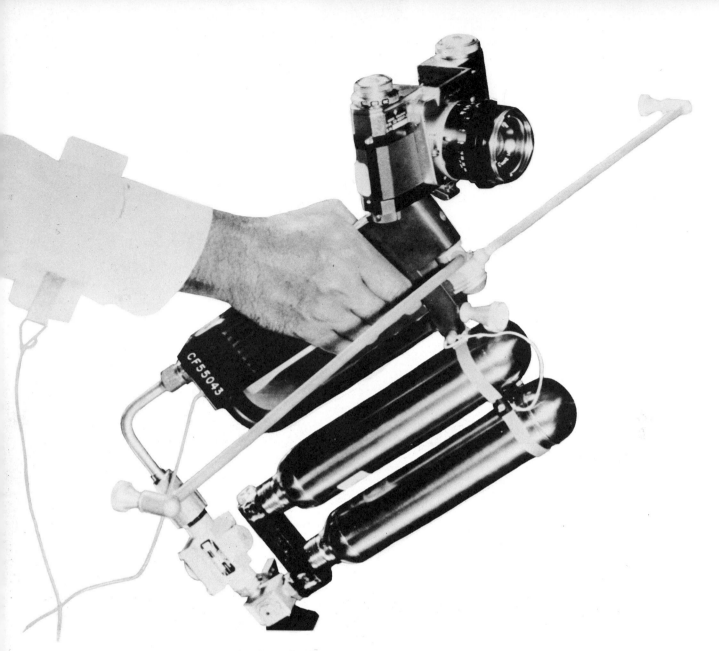

H is for Hand-Held Maneuvering Unit (called HHMU)

a little rocket engine that an astronaut holds in his hand and shoots like a gun. When it fires in one direction, the astronaut goes in the other. He can move around in space outside the ship that way.

h is for heatshield

a metal cover on the bottom of the
spaceship. This shield gets most of the
heat when the spaceship moves very fast.
It keeps the ship from burning up when it
comes back into the Earth's air. The
astronauts stay cool inside the spaceship. **19**

I is for Ignition

catching fire. When fuel and oxygen mix, an electric spark can make them ignite. Burning starts, and the engine begins to work. When this happens with a rocket engine, fiery exhaust gases shoot out of the base and the spaceship slowly begins to move upward.

i is for interstellar space

_____

_____

_____

the empty area between the stars. There is hardly any air in interstellar space, or anything else to stop starlight. Stars can be seen clearly even when they are far, far away.

J is for Jupiter

the largest planet. It is eleven times as wide across its middle (that is, its diameter) as the Earth is. It has twelve moons going around it. It is the second brightest planet. Venus is the brightest. Some day astronauts may take a long, long, long trip to study Jupiter from close up.

j is for jet

the stream of fire and gas that shoots out of a rocket engine. This jet goes in one direction, and the spaceship moves in the opposite direction. When the jet moves downward, the spaceship lifts upward.

K is for Kennedy Space Center

where spaceships take off. It is on the coast of Florida. Before men planned to go to the Moon, Cape Kennedy was a quiet spot on the seashore. Now it is one of the busiest and most exciting places in the world.

k is for kinetic energy

the force that makes a moving object do things a motionless one cannot do. A moving baseball will break a window. A motionless baseball can't. Spaceships go fast enough to build up a lot of kinetic energy. That helps them push into space against the downward pull of Earth's gravity.

23

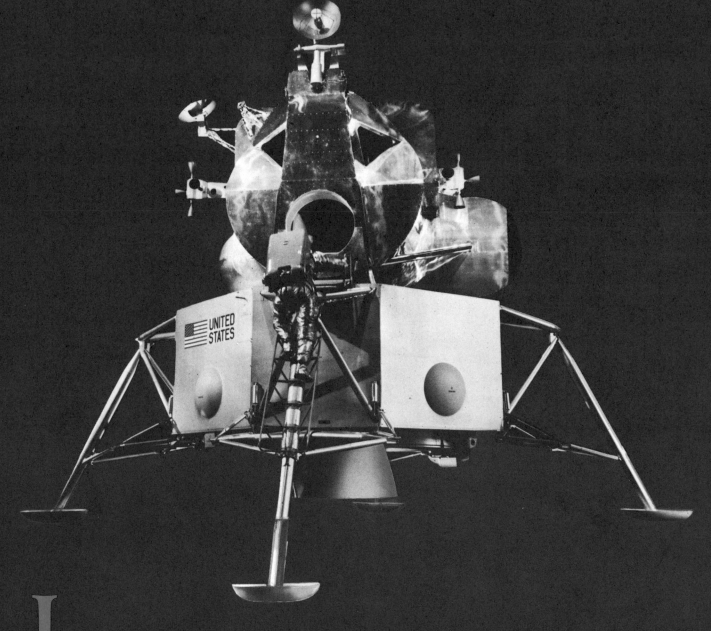

L is for Lunar Module

_____

_____

_____

a little spaceship that takes two astronauts from Apollo to land on the Moon. It has long, thin metal legs to stand **24** on, so it is sometimes called a spider.

1 is for lift-off

the beginning of the flight into space. The fuel and the oxygen mix and ignite. There is a streak of fire coming out below. The spaceship lifts off the pad. First it moves slowly. Then it goes faster and faster.

M is for Moon

_____

_____

_____

the Earth's companion world or satellite. It takes the
Moon about twenty-eight days to go around the Earth.
As the Moon turns into sunlight and into darkness, each
spot stays very hot for two weeks, then very cold for two
weeks. It is the closest globe to the Earth and is smaller
than the Earth. It is the first world in space where
astronauts have landed.

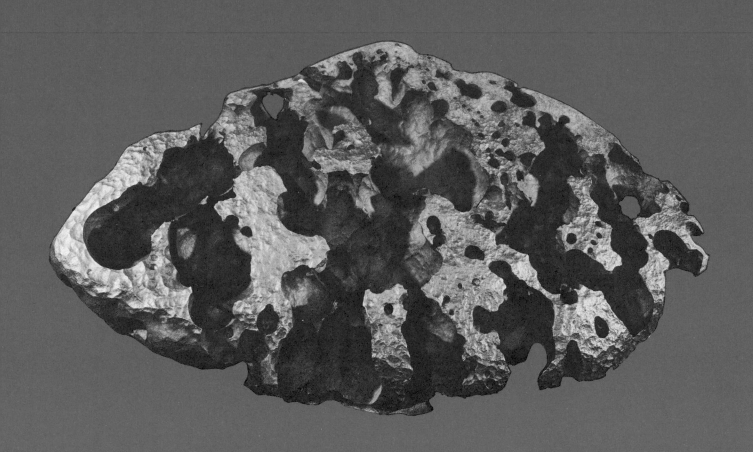

m is for meteor

_____

_____

_____

a piece of matter that whizzes through space. Some
meteors come into the Earth's air and heat up. Then they
glow with light. When we see them, we call them
shooting stars. They usually turn into gas, but
sometimes one comes to Earth. It seems like a very
hard, rough piece of metal or rock, and is called a
meteorite.

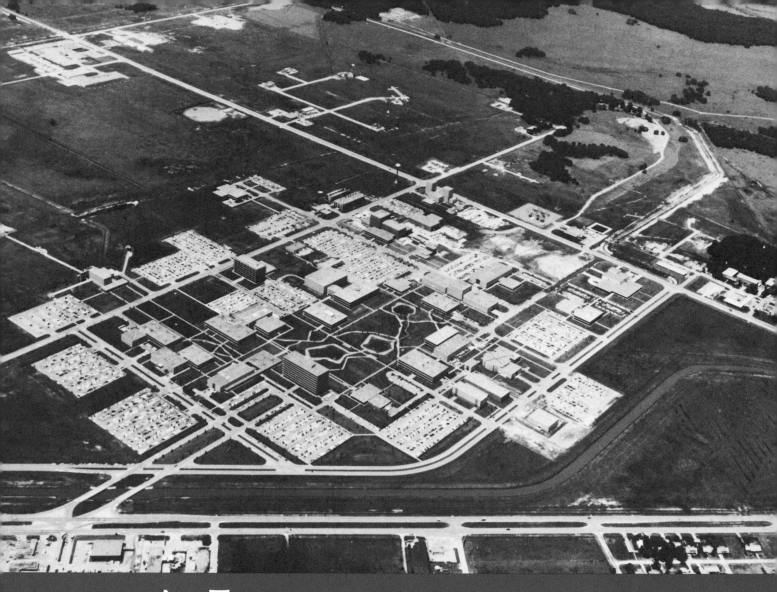

N is for NASA

the government organization—the National Aeronautics
and Space Administration—that runs the space program.
It started work in 1958 after the first United States
Earth satellites were launched. The control and
communications center for all of the launches is in
Houston, Texas.

28

n is for nosecone

a smooth metal covering at the tip of a spaceship. When the ship goes through the Earth's air, it could get too hot. The smooth nosecone slips through the air easily. Less heat is formed and the astronauts stay cool inside. Out in space, the nosecone falls away.

O is for Ocean of Storms

a dark, smooth area on the Moon where the first unmanned spaceship landed in 1966. It is not really an ocean, because there is probably no water on the Moon. There are no storms either, but we still use the name.

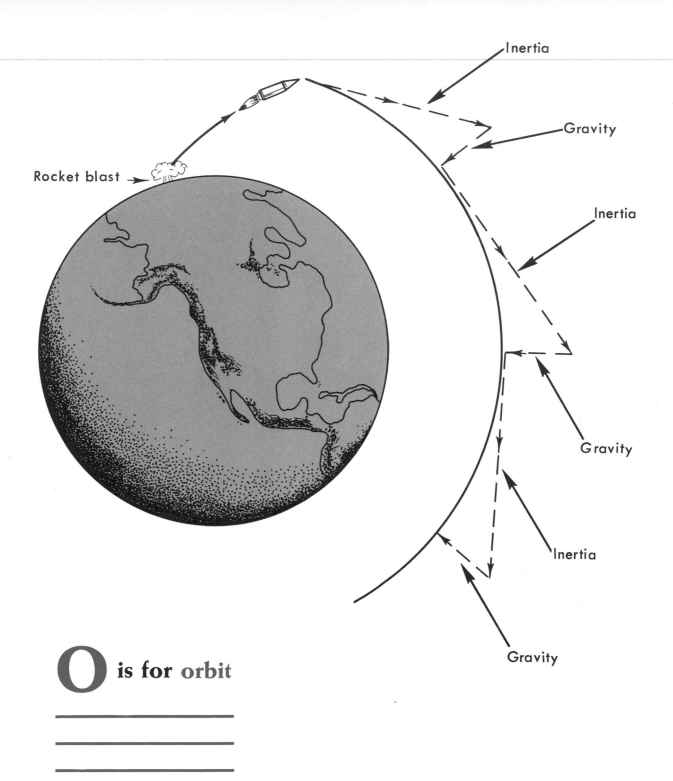

Inertia

Gravity

Inertia

Rocket blast →

Gravity

Inertia

Gravity

O is for orbit

_____

_____

_____

the path a small world takes around a larger one. The
Moon moves in an orbit around the Earth. The Earth
moves in an orbit around the Sun. Both orbits are almost
like circles. An orbit is also the path a spaceship takes
around the Earth or the Moon.

31

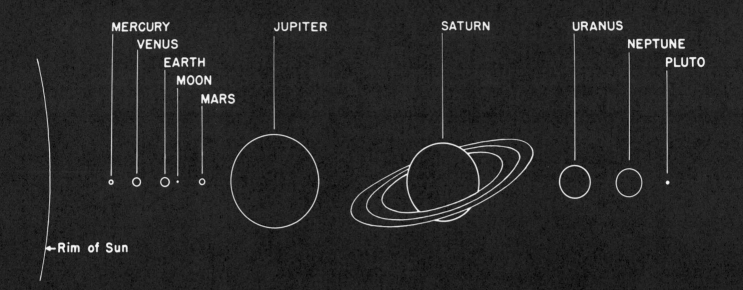

MERCURY
VENUS
EARTH
MOON
MARS
JUPITER
SATURN
URANUS
NEPTUNE
PLUTO

←Rim of Sun

RELATIVE DIAMETERS OF THE PLANETS

P is for Planet

any world that moves around the Sun. The Earth is a
planet, but the Moon is not one. Mars, Venus, Jupiter,
and Saturn are planets. Altogether there are nine planets
that move around the Sun. Someday astronauts will go
long distances in spaceships to explore the planets.

32

P is for payload

the part of a spaceship that holds men and instruments. Most of a spaceship is taken up by tanks of fuel and oxygen. The part that holds the astronauts and the instruments does the real work. That's the part that "pays off."

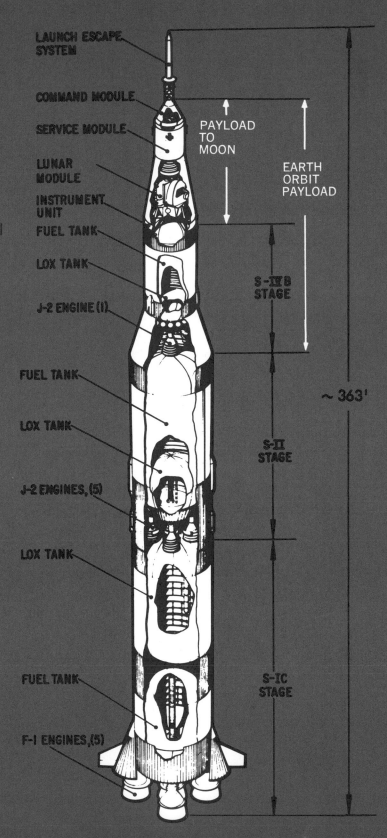

LAUNCH ESCAPE SYSTEM

COMMAND MODULE

SERVICE MODULE

LUNAR MODULE

INSTRUMENT UNIT

FUEL TANK

LOX TANK

J-2 ENGINE (I)

FUEL TANK

LOX TANK

J-2 ENGINES, (5)

LOX TANK

FUEL TANK

F-I ENGINES, (5)

PAYLOAD TO MOON

EARTH ORBIT PAYLOAD

S-IVB STAGE

S-II STAGE

S-IC STAGE

~ 363'

SATURN V

Q is for Quark

the smallest object anyone has talked about in science. Scientists think that all the parts inside an atom may be made up of Quarks. No one has ever found signs that Quarks really exist, so this picture is still to be filled in. Perhaps in studying space, astronauts may find some.

q is for quasar

a mysterious object, brighter and farther away than anything else we can see. Scientists still don't know what quasars are. Maybe astronauts will be able to make tests from the Moon that will help to explain them.

R is for Rocket

something that is moved by jet. A Fourth of July rocket has a small supply of gunpowder. When the gunpowder burns, a jet of gas shoots down and sends the rocket into the air. The engines of jet airplanes work the same way. Spaceships are very large rockets. They lift far up until they are out of the Earth's air and into space.

r is for reentry

coming back to earth from outer space where there is no air at all. A spaceship must enter the air around the Earth without burning up completely. It has to stay in the thin upper air until it slows down. Then it can enter the thicker air closer to the ground for a landing.

35

S is for Satellite

_____

any object that travels around a planet.

The Moon is the Earth's satellite. When a

spaceship is sent into orbit around the

Earth, it becomes a man-made satellite.

The first man-made satellite was sent into space

36 in 1957 by the Russians. It was called Sputnik I.

S is for splashdown

————————————
————————————
————————————

a spaceship landing at sea. It is safer to come to Earth
in water than on dry land. The collision is not as hard,
just as it hurts less to fall into a swimming pool from a
diving board than to fall to the ground from a tree.
Helicopters pick the astronauts out of the sea and fly
them to a Navy aircraft carrier waiting nearby.

T is for Terminator

the line where the darkness begins on the Moon, or on any other world. The Sun lights up only the half of the Moon that faces it. The rest of the Moon is dark. Its terminator is sharp because the Moon has no air to spread the light around. The Earth's terminator is fuzzy because there's enough air to spread the light.

t is for thrust

the push upward that a jet gives a spaceship. The
thrust must be great enough to send the ship far into
space. Today's large spaceships have enough thrust to
carry astronauts to the Moon.

39

U is for Universe.

everything there is. It is the Earth and the Moon and all the stars. It is all the space between the stars, too, as far as you can imagine. Astronauts will help us to learn more about the Universe.

U is for umbilical

_____

_____

_____

the rope that holds an astronaut to his
ship when he is moving about in space.
There is no gravity to hold him to the ship.
Without the rope he might drift so far
away that he could not get back.

V is for Voyager

a spaceship that will some day go from the Earth to the
planet Mars. Mars is much farther from the Earth than
the Moon is. There will be no men on Voyager. It will
carry instruments to send back information about Mars.
This picture shows how men many years ago thought of
the first ships that would go out to the Moon and other

V is for vacuum

space that has nothing in it, not even air. There is no air in outer space, nor on the Moon. If an astronaut leaves his ship he must wear a special spacesuit. It has a supply of oxygen for him to breathe. Without it he could not live.

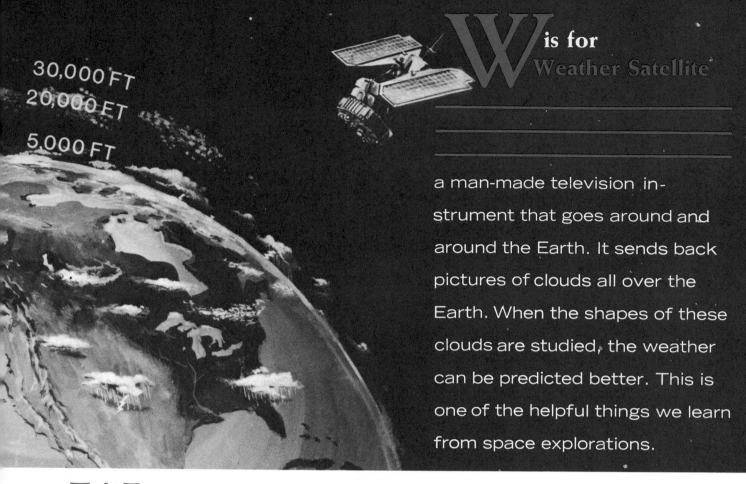

30,000 FT
20,000 FT
5,000 FT

W is for Weather Satellite

a man-made television instrument that goes around and around the Earth. It sends back pictures of clouds all over the Earth. When the shapes of these clouds are studied, the weather can be predicted better. This is one of the helpful things we learn from space explorations.

W is for white room

the place where the astronauts wait just before take-off. It has white walls, and the men in it wear white coats. Everything is kept as clean as possible, to make sure that no dirt or germs get into the spaceship with

44 the astronauts.

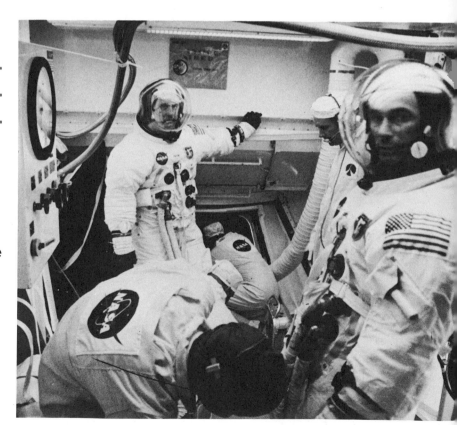

X is for X ray

a form of light we can't see but which can be very harmful. The X rays that come from the Sun are stopped by the Earth's air. Unmanned spaceships will probably be able to find out about them. Then maybe we will understand better how to protect astronauts from them. This is a picture of the Sun photographed in X rays.

X is for experimental

a kind of test. Before any complicated new thing can be done, it must be tried out in a simple way. The first modern rocket was a small one fired in 1926. It is shown here with the man who invented it, Robert H. Goddard.

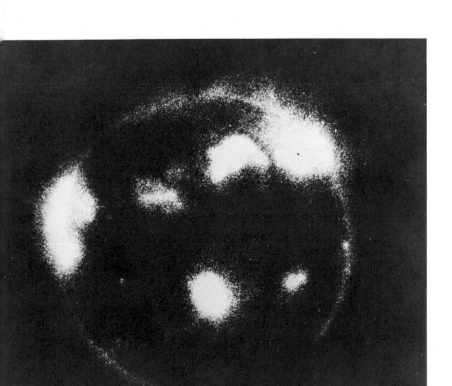

Yaw

Roll

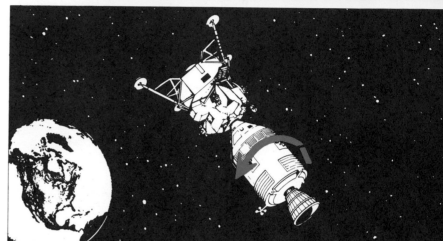

Pitch

Y is for Yaw

a kind of wobble. Spaceships can wobble in three ways.
The ends can move from side to side, which is a "yaw."
The ends can move up and down, which is a "pitch." Or
the entire spaceship can "roll." Astronauts try to prevent
these motions because they make it hard to study the

worlds in space.

Y is for year

the time it takes a planet to go around the Sun. The Earth's year is 365 days long. Mars has a longer year because it is farther away from the Sun. Venus has a shorter one because it is closer to the Sun.

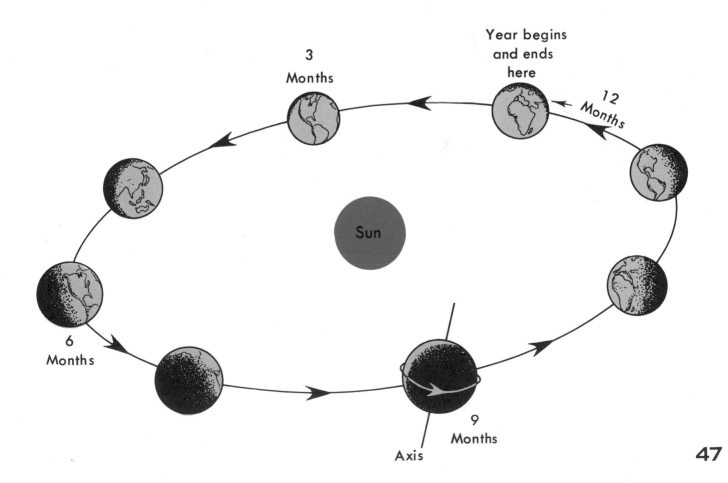

47

Z is for Zond

a large Russian spaceship. Zond ships have traveled very far out from the Earth. One went around the Moon. Another one passed close to Mars. But they did not have astronauts aboard. They carried a lot of instruments to find out more about space.

Z is for zero gravity

what astronauts live with when their spaceship moves after the rockets have been shut off. Astronauts feel no pull then. They can float in air or stand upside down. It is hard to drink water if it floats in air. Astronauts have to suck it out of a container.